D1560204

EX Libris

Blanche Williams Hull

A LITTLE HISTORY OF
THE HORN-BOOK

A LITTLE HISTORY OF

The Horn-book

By
BEULAH FOLMSBEE

THE HORN BOOK, *Inc.*
BOSTON

Introduction

ALTHOUGH definitions of the horn-book bear a considerable degree of sameness, there are still many, and sometimes amusing, conjectures as to the meaning of the word. Elsewhere in this little history there have been printed some definitions and allusions culled from sources spanning more than six centuries; indeed, those to whom the general history of the horn-book is known may well skip these earlier pages which have been written for those who start from scratch — who, to put it in words more consonant with our subject, are not yet out of the criss-cross row of their learning.

This is perhaps as good a place as any to say that the material presented in these pages has grown out of inquiries made over a period of years by readers of *The Horn Book Magazine* — so named because it is concerned solely with children's books and reading. A further reason for this brief study might also be found in the fact that the writer has herself sought enlightenment on many questions raised during the pleasant task of making some reproductions of the hornbook and its next of kin, the battledore; those who may desire information beyond all bounds of a very primer such as this can do no better than to consult Tuer's *History of the Horn-book* and the other sources, given in the closing pages, to which she is indebted for the answers to most of them. And now,

> " Christe's crosse be my spede,
> In all vertue to proceed."

B. F.

June, 1942.

THE horn-book was the earliest lesson-book made for children to use themselves. To be sure, as some writers on the subject have pointed out, the horn-book was not a "book" at all in the common understanding of that word. However, if one of the meanings given in the newest edition of Webster's may be taken as the more inclusive definition, the horn-book was indeed well named:

book: *anything that may be studied like a book*

Certainly the horn-book was made to be studied, and certain it is that its horn covering was used not to enhance its beauty or to keep it spotlessly clean *until*, as in the case of the omnipresent cellophane-wrapped items of today, it could, after valiant struggle by the purchaser, be removed and the article within put to the use for which it was purchased; no, the horn was applied so that the lesson-sheet might be saved from some of the wear and tear and grubby finger marks which were sure to follow *after* its delivery into the hands of its young owner.

The horn-book, then, was the first book made for children themselves to handle. The simplest, and therefore the one most commonly used, was composed of a piece of wood cut in the shape of a paddle in a size convenient for holding in the hand[1]; on one side was pasted the lesson-sheet, and over this was laid a piece of transparent horn which was held in place by narrow brass strips tacked through the horn (and probably through the edges of the lesson-sheet as well) to the wood. Sometimes a hole was bored in the handle so that a cord or leather thong could be strung through it and hung about the neck, or suspended from the girdle or wrist. Although no such actual reference has come to light during the compilation of this material, boys were not boys in those

---

[1] The size varied, of course, but true *horn*-books (see page 10) in general use were approximately 2¾ x 5″ (including the handle) or even smaller.

*A horn-book of the kind commonly
used in almost perfect condition*

early days if some horn-books did not carry the crudely carved initials of their owners, together with sundry other youthful markings; the time-honored " picture of teacher " was probably not indulged in for obvious reasons.

Just as books printed from movable types brought about many variations from the manuscript volumes and the block-printed books of the days before the " invention of printing " so, in the horn-book, there were changes and variations growing out of the developments of materials and processes, as well as many degrees of quality — this latter expressed largely in the cheapness or fineness of materials and workmanship, since the lesson-sheet itself shows little or no variation whether for princeling or potboy. Thus we find that horn-books were made not only of wood, but of ivory, various metals, leather, cardboard, and even of gingerbread,[1] and that they ranged from the plain, whittled kind to elaborately carved wood specimens, and to the tooled, embossed, and engraved

---

[1] Not, of course, of the "gingerbread-and-whipped-cream" variety, but of a consistency more like those cookies known as "ginger snaps."

"limited editions," a few of which are
shown in the illustrations to be found in
these pages.

THE LESSON-SHEET

The lesson-sheet itself may be described in
few words. Of vellum or parchment in the
earliest specimens, later of paper, it was hand-
written or printed from type as follows:
first, the ✠ (Christ's cross, Christ-cross,
Criss-cross, etc.) followed by as much of the
alphabet in small letters as the space would
permit — hence the " criss-cross row," or the
beginning of learning.

" Now we in the country beginne and goe forward
with our reading in this manner *Christs Crosse* be
my Speed, and the Holy Ghost: for feare the
Divell should be in the letters of the Alphabet, as
hee is too often when he teacheth od fellowes to
play tricks with their creditors, who instead of pay-
ments, write I O U, and so scoffe many an honest
man out of his goods."

> —*The Court and Country, or a Brief Dis-
> course between the Courtier and Country-
> man: of the Manner, Nature and Condition
> of their lives, etc.* Written by N. B., Gent.,
> London. Printed by G. Eld for John Wright,
> and are to be sold at his Shoppe at the Signe
> of the Bible without Newgate, 1618

Cros and curteis Crist, this begynnynge Spede!
Piers the Plowman's Crede, 14th Century

In the morenynge whan ye up rise
To worshipe gode have in memorie,
Wyth *crystes crosse* loke ye blesse you Christ,
Your pater noster saye in devoute wyse,
Ave maria with the holy crede,
Thenne alle the day the better shal ye spede.

Book of Curtesye (circa 1477)

Clarence: (George, Duke of Clarence)

Yea, Richard, when I know; for I protest
As yet I do not: but, as I can learn,
He hearkens after prophecies and dreams;
And from the *cross-row* plucks the letter G
And says a wizard told him that by G
His issues disinherited should be:
And, for my name of George begins with G,
It follows in his thought that I am he.

Shakespeare, *Richard III*, Act I, Scene 1

And if you know
The *Christ-Cross-Row,*
You soon may Spell and read;
In this smooth Way
From Day to Day
You will run on with Speed.

Ronksley's *Child's Weeke-work* (1712)

An amusing application of the cross row
is found in an illustration on the title page
of *The Old Egyptian Fortune Teller's Last*

6

Legacy, a chapbook in the British Museum. This intricate " lover's knot " untied reads as follows:

A ✛ begins Love's Cris ✛ Row,
Love's not without A ✛ or two.
A double ✛ begins this knot.
Without ✛es Merit is not.
This Knot and Love are both alike,
Whose first and last are both to seek
No ✛ can stay true Love's intent
It still goes on to What is ment
And though it Meats with many A one
True Love makes a ✛ seem none.
He that loves must Learn to know
A ✛ begins Love's Cris ✛ Row.

Followed then the rest of the alphabet in small letters; the alphabet in capitals; the vowels; the vowels in combination with the consonants (after them, sometimes, the nine digits); the Exorcism, and The Lord's Prayer. Evidence of the antiquity of the lesson text may be seen in the ending of The Lord's Prayer with " deliver us from Evil " according to the practice of the Roman Church. In this connection it should be pointed out that certain lesson-sheets, probably some of those printed during the reign of Elizabeth and the first two Stuarts, omitted the cross and added to the prayer, " For thyne is the kingdome," etc. (See illustration on page 28.) These were no doubt for the Puritan Sectaries of whom Morton wrote in 1632 (in his *New English Canaan*) that a " Silenced Minister," who came over to New England, brought

a great Bundell of Horne books with him, and careful hee was (good man) to blott out all the crosses of them for feare least the people of the land should become Idolaters.

Sometimes, too, the entire lesson was surrounded by a decorative border made of type

A a b c d e f g h i k l m n o p q
r s t u b w x y z. & e i o u.
A B C D E F G H I K L M N
O P Q R S T U W X Y Z.

a e i o u	a e i o u
ab eb ib ob ub	ba ce bi bo bu
ae ec ic oc ue	ca ce ci co cu
ad ed id od ud	da de di do du

In the name of the Father, & of the
Son, & of the Holy Ghost, Amen.

Our Father which art in heaven, hallowed be thy Name.
Thy kingdom come. Thy will
be done in Earth, as it is in Heaven. Give us this day our daily
bread. And forgive us our trespas-
ses, as we forgive them that trespass
against us. And lead us not into
temptation. But deliver us from
evil, Amen.

This black-letter lesson-sheet is one
of sixteen printed on a single sheet
of paper, in the Bagford Collection
(British Museum)

ornaments; of this, more will be said later.

Such, then, was the lesson-sheet of the true horn-book; that is to say, the horn-book in which a sheet of horn was employed for the purpose of protecting the lesson-sheet, and which was peculiar to English-speaking peoples. As various kinds of lesson tablets have been in use from the earliest days and the demarcation between these and the horn-books of later days often too lightly passed over, it will be well to include Tuer's admirable brief summary of the history of the recorded word as given in his *History of the Horn-Book,* especially as its quotation here leads naturally to the interesting subjects of horn, paper, and printing types as they were used in the making of horn-books.

In days when human history was unwittingly written in the flints and potsherds which mother earth has so faithfully treasured for us, man's earliest attempts at writing must have been signs and pictures drawn in the sand or roughly scratched on wood or stone. As time advanced, thoughts were more conveniently impressed on the inner bark of trees, and later, on papyrus, and wooden, wax-covered folding *tabulæ.* "Write the vision and make it plain upon tables, that he may run that readeth it." Still later, when papyrus was super-

✠ A a b c d e f g h i j k l m n o p q
r ſ s t u v w x y z &   a e i o u
A B C D E F G H I J K L M N O P Q
R S T U V W X Y Z

a e i o u	a e i o u
ab eb ib ob ub	ba be bi bo bu
ac ec ic oc uc	ca ce ci co cu
ad ed id od ud	da de di do du

In the Name of the Father and of the
Son, and of the Holy Ghoſt. *Amen.*

OUR Father, which art in
Heaven, hallowed be thy
Name; thy Kingdom come, thy
Will be done on Earth, as it is in
Heaven. Give us this Day our
daily Bread; and forgive us our
Treſpaſſes, as we forgive them
that treſpaſs againſt us ; And
lead us not into Temptation, but
deliver us from Evil.   *Amen.*

*Lesson-sheet set by hand from old
type in 1939 by the printers of the
Horn Book Magazine*

seded by parchment and vellum, but in days far behind the invention of paper and printing, the horn-book was the happy thought of an overtaxed scribe, who, heartily detesting the profitless labour of rewriting the A B C, fastened the skin to a slab of wood and covered it with horn.

The horn-book proper — of which a sheet of horn forms a component part — is peculiar to English-speaking peoples. It has been extensively used here and in America, but never in other countries. The horn-book that we see in old Continental engravings is simply an alphabetical tablet without the protection of horn.

The use of translucent horn having been universal, it is possible, of course, that foreign specimens of the horn-book protected with horn may yet be discovered. It is quite certain, however, that the horn-book as we know it was never in general use elsewhere than in England and America.

That numbers of horn-books were brought to America, or sent here from England, is known from early records and account books. The following interesting extract is from a rare folio preserved among the *Americana*, in the library of Harvard College, entitled: —

THE | GENERAL ACCOMPT | OF ALL | MONIES and EFFECTS | Received and Expended by the TRUSTEES | For Establishing the Colony of | *GEORGIA* in *AMERICA;* | etc.

EFFECTS received in *England* within the Time of this Accompt, from the several Persons hereafter mentioned, and applied by the Trustees.

	Names of Contributors.	Effects contributed.
1735. *July,* 6 Ditto	A Person who desires to be unknown, by the Hands of the Reverend Dr. *Hales,* for the Use of the New Settlement which is going to be made at the Southward Part of GEORGIA . .	One Bible, *4to.* One Common Prayer Book, *4to.* Twenty Bibles, Minion *12mo.* Twenty five Testaments, Long Primer *8vo.* Fifty Common Prayer Books, Minion *12mo.* Twenty five Bishop of Man, on the Lord's Supper. Fifty Christian Monitor, and Companion to the Altar. Fifty Christian Monitor, and Answer to Excuses. One hundred Horn-Books. One hundred Primers. One hundred A, B, C, with the Church Catechism.

In *Salem Imprints,* by Harriet S. Tapley, there is mention that " Edward Hilliard purchased a horn-book for 4d " from George Corwin, a Salem merchant, sometime before 1685. The Diary of Samuel Sewall carries an entry, " 27th April, 1691. This after-

noon had Joseph to school to Capt. Town-
send's Mother's, his cousin Jane accompany-
ing him, carried his hornbook."

HORN

The question almost invariably first raised
by the tyro, as concerns the subject of horn-
books, has to do with the source and pro-
curement of the horn which sets these lesson
books apart from all others. Most of the
learned professors and the collectors of horn-
books (both those writing at a time when
animals might be seen in the course of any
day's normal pursuits, instead of, as now, on
occasional trips to the country or the zoo,
and those who, in more recent years, have
no notion of doing our research for us) dis-
miss the subject of horn with a mere reference to its being "obtained from the horns
of cattle, sheep, goats, etc." Surely the Wor-
shipful Company of Horners of London,
whose Fairs were held at least as early as the
time of Henry III, and whose trade "put
the horn in hornbook," deserve a paragraph
or two. Here, then, is a recipe for making
horn leaves (which is the name by which the

thin sheets were known) for " Lanthorns, as now used by farmers in Yorkshire," and " for covering horn-books."

The peculiar texture of horn, its toughness and agreeable natural colors, have always caused it to be a favorite material for many works, though the increasing cheapness of glass, gutta percha and metal wares has caused a great disuse of it. At one time there was held in England a fair at which every object for sale was made of horn.

As true horn consists, chemically, of albumen (keratin) and a little prosphate of lime, it is readily softened in boiling water or by heat; sometimes the process is aided by the addition of quicklime. It is usual to prepare the horns of oxen and sheep by steeping them for several weeks in cold water, which has the effect of separating the cored bony part from the cover of true horn. The latter is then heated, first for half an hour in boiling water, and then over a fire. In this condition it may be cut or molded with great ease.

To make sheets for lanterns or combs, the horn is slit lengthways at the side, heated and pressed out, either between plates or by machines, of which several have been invented. Care must, however, be exercised as to the application of both heat and pressure since, owing to its peculiarly laminated structure and the striæ abounding through it . . . horn has a tendency to split.

The author confesses that the directions above (for which she is indebted to the *Universal Cyclopædia and Atlas*) are given in full with the hope that some kindred soul living in cattle country and endowed with the spirit of adventure will try them out and by some happy chance send her a sheet or two of real horn to use in place of the synthetic materials now employed by her in the making of reproductions (see page 58). A horn-book, my masters, in trade for some leaves of horn! And so to some considerations of paper, the scarcity of which brought about the use of

The faithful Horn before, from age to age,
Preserving thy invaluable Page.

PAPER

The earliest of the horn-book lesson-sheets were undoubtedly written by hand on parchment (skin of sheep or goats, etc.) or vellum (fine-grained lambskin, kidskin, etc.). Later came the use of paper, but as this, in the earliest days of its use, was imported and expensive, the device of covering it with horn came into being, as we have seen. Not until 1494 was paper manufactured in England.

It may be well to note here for those

Horn-book covered with brickdust-colored paper. Printed on the back is the decoration shown on page 57

whose interests have not led them into the fascinating study of the material which played so great a part in the development of communication by means of the printed word, that paper was first invented in China, about 105 A. D. Elsewhere in this little history will be found a reference to the decline of the horn-book and the rise, as paper became less expensive, of the cardboard and paper battledores. In order that the phrase " as paper became less expensive " (used by most horn-book historians and gratefully adopted by this one) may have fuller meaning, a simple map is here included to show paper's thousand-and-more years' journey from China to Europe and thence across the sea to America where it was first manufactured in 1690, at Philadelphia. The figures on the map (except those in Chinese Turkestan) represent the earliest recorded *local manufacture* of paper. In many cases the earliest *import* of paper preceded the earliest local manufacture by from one to two centuries.

Indeed, the first record of paper making in the United States seems to be a sentence from a letter, sent in 1690 from Pennsylvania by William Bradford, printer, to a friend in London: " Samuel Carpenter and I are Building a Paper-Mill about a Mile from thy Mills

Sixteenth-century woodcut by Jost Amman showing a paper maker at work

at Skulkill, and hope we shall have Paper within less than four months."

From the foregoing paragraphs and the map, which have skipped with such seeming disregard of time and distance from the China of an early Christian era to the days of Colonial America, the reader will, it is hoped, have gained some interesting side-lights on an essential part of the horn-book. The lesson-sheet and its horn covering having been briefly dealt with, a glance at the description of a simple horn-book given on page 2 will disclose that two other factors have yet to be discussed; the brass strips, or "lattens," as they were called, which were used to cover the edges of the horn, and the hand-forged tacks which held them in place.

LATTENS AND TACKS

Latten is a kind of brass or brass-like alloy hammered into thin sheets which may easily be cut with ordinary scissors. According to the dictionary, it was "formerly much used for church utensils," which may be one of the reasons why the makers of horn-books chose it as a suitable frame for a lesson-sheet in which The Lord's Prayer occupies well over half the space.

He had a cross of latoun full of stones.
— *Chaucer*

The tacks used in early horn-books were hand-forged and known as rose-head, or Flemish, tacks. As will be seen in the illustration (much enlarged), the head of the tack has been hammered to make four facets which converge to make a boss at the top, thus protecting the horn from scratches when the horn-book was laid face down. Hand-forged tacks, Tuer reminds us, passed as currency in many northern villages of England as late as the middle of the eighteenth century, but the rose-head tack was to a large extent replaced by the flat-headed and machine-made tacks about 1820. In making the reproductions referred to on page 58, the writer sought far and wide for tacks small enough and irregular enough in shape to suggest those used in real horn-books of an early date; the best substitutes that could be found were some which had been discarded by the manufacturer because of uneven size and battered-looking heads. Of these, alas, there was but a precious handful, for the type of which they were the outcasts was no longer being made. If, by chance, some reader of these pages possesses one of the reproductions with these "imperfect" tacks, let him cherish it the more, for it approaches the original more closely than any made since this early supply gave out.

Reference has been made to horn-books in which the wood has been given a special decorative treatment — by carving, or by covering with various materials — but as we are concerned mainly with the horn-book in common use, we shall take time to construct here, by word and sketch, a horn-book such as might have been made for a good little girl of the eighteenth century — or such as *you* might make (approximately) in the twentieth!

1. A piece of wood, generally oak, measuring about 2¾ x 5 inches, whittled into the shape of a paddle or batlet.

2. The lesson, printed in type of the period (see pages 9 and 11) surrounded by a printed border,[1] and pasted to the wood with a piece of horn laid over it.

3. The brass strips, about ⅛ inch wide, tacked lightly at the centers, leaving the ends loose so that corners can later be matched and trimmed.

4. The strips trimmed at the ends to form square corners, and the tacks driven in to complete a horn-book which sold for three halfpence.

---

[1] It should be noted that the border was often entirely covered by the latten so that it is possible its use was as much for the purpose of providing a guide for the latten as for any decorative purpose. The lattens were often carelessly and probably hastily applied without much rhyme or reason in the lapping of the corners. Some reproductions of old horn-books show no border at all except where the lattens have disappeared; in others, the border shows on one or two sides only—a pity, since in most cases it added a pleasant decoration to this early lesson book.

The variations in books currently published — in size, shape, design, decoration and binding — have their counterparts in the horn-books of our ancestors. There are in the world today, in the possession of fortunate private collectors, libraries and museums, horn-books of various kinds. As mentioned earlier, there were even horn-books of gingerbread, though needless to say, of these there remain today only the molds. Before turning to the pages on which may be seen illustrations of some of these horn-books, together with brief descriptive notes, a word must be said on the provocative question of types used in the printing of horn-book lesson-sheets, and their relation to the probable dates of the various horn-books in existence.

TYPES — *Black-Letter and Roman*

It is probable that true horn-books, in the earliest period of their use in England, were written in manuscript and it is likely that the hand-written form persisted even after printing became fairly common. The illustration on page 25 is of a manuscript horn-

*The only manuscript horn-book
in the Plimpton Collection*

book in the collection of the late George A.
Plimpton, who owned, in all, twenty-four
horn-books, most of which were found in
England. The earliest of the printed horn-
books were, of course, in black-letter, but as
any beginner in the history of typography will

know, the use of black-letter does not set the date of the printed page. Types stored away for a century or more may well have been unearthed from their dusty bins and put to work again even after black-letter had been dealt its death blow by the beautiful Roman types which came into use and flourished during the sixteenth century — Typography's Golden Age.

From the time of Gutenberg (beginning about 1450, until the year 1625) printers cast their own types. In the year 1637 England enforced a decree limiting the number of typefounders to four. Types were cast exclusively by hand. (See illustration on page 27.) Without doubt some of the earliest horn-books to be printed in Roman type stemmed from the workshop of John Daye, whose beautiful fonts of Roman and Italic type were cast by himself and his workmen about 1567, for he is known to have issued books in which the title pages are set in Roman and Italic, carrying the imprint, " At London, printed by John Daye, dwelling over Aldersgate, 1570." Generally speaking, then, the earliest printed horn-

books used black-letter — a type which was
based on the style of lettering used by copyists
when making manuscript books, and to

Making type in the sixteenth century
From a woodcut by Jost Amman

which we often refer as " Old English " or
" Gothic," its pointed strokes suggesting the
prominent features of Gothic Architecture.
As has been suggested earlier, hand-written

Aabcdefghiklmnop
qrꝛſstuvwxyz,:.

ABCDEFGHIKLMN
OPQRSTVWXYZ

ab eb ib ob vb an en in on vn
ac ec ic oc vc ap ep ip op vp
ad ed id od vd ar er ir oꝛ vꝛ

In the Name of GOD the
Father, the Son, and of
the holy Ghost: So be it.

OUr Father, which art in Heaven, Halowed be thy Name:
Thy kingdome come: Thy Will
be done in Earth, as it is in Heaven: Giue vs this day our daylie
Bread: And foꝛgiue vs our tres-
passes, as wee foꝛgiue them that
trespasse against vs: And leade vs
not into temptation, But deliuer
vs from Euill : Foꝛ thyne is the
kingdome, Power, and Gloꝛie
foꝛ euer, and euer, So be it.

Printed in Aberdeen by E. Raban
probably about 1620. Note the ab-
sence of the criss-cross

horn-books were probably made and used by the die-hards long after printing in black-letter type had become the practice; just so it is likely that printers of the sixteenth and seventeenth centuries continued to use their black-letter faces long after Roman came into common use. He would be a daring person indeed who attempted to place, within a century or two of the mark, the date of a black-letter horn-book. But as Roman type-faces are known to have come into use for the first time about fifteen years after the invention of printing, that is about 1470, and more Roman type-faces than any others were used by 1580, it may at least be said that horn-books with the lesson-sheet printed in Roman types date possibly from the fifteenth century, but certainly not before that time.

Down through not years, then, but centuries, the horn-book fulfilled its mission of teaching children their letters until developments in paper-making, printing and engraving brought about the manufacture of paper battledores, chapbooks, primers, and the " pretty little pocket-books " bound in their

A leather-covered horn-book dating
from about the time of James I, the
back stamped with a favorite device,
St. George and the Dragon

"flowery and gilt" (in which eighteenth century moralizing gave way to tales of action and adventure) issued by John Newbery from his shop in St. Paul's Churchyard.

Brass stamping block of St. George and the Dragon shown at about one-quarter its actual size

Some Notes on Battledores

"Horn-Books are now so completely superseded by the Battledore and the various forms of Reading made Easy that they are rarely met with, and few persons believe that such was formerly the means adopted to teach the infantine ideas how to shoot."

So reads the opening paragraph of an article on horn-books published in Willis's

Current Notes for October, 1855. The battledore referred to in the quotation was of the paper or cardboard kind illustrated on page 39, but as "battledore" and "horn-book" were often used  interchangeably in reference to the purposes which both, as lesson-books, served, rather than to their physical similarity, a few notes to explain the derivation will not be amiss.

The word "battledore" has its counterpart in the French *battoir*, the Portuguese *batidor*, the Spanish *batidero* and the Old English *batyldoure*, all of these signifying a stout board or paddle used by washerwomen to beat their clothes clean. It would be difficult to state when such an implement first came into use, but one may hazard the guess that it followed close upon the heels of the first washable garments, and in certain parts of the world today it is still in use. It is equally difficult to ascertain when children discovered the pleasures of a game in which a bit of something could be batted about with such a wooden paddle or batlet; certain it is that such a " play thing " may be found in infinite variety today — from highly specialized racquets to the " bouncers " on toy counters in the five-and-ten-cent stores; the currently popular game of badminton is but the outgrowth of the game of Battledore and Shuttlecock played for centuries past in the Orient.

In the course of searching through the various books and periodicals listed at the close of this Little History, an interesting bit of information about the battledores which were used in the early game of *La Longue Paûme* came to light and it is shared here with those who, like this writer, have wondered about the use of the word " battledore " as applied to the folded paper lesson-book which superseded the horn-book.

In about 1380 Chaucer wrote, in " Troylus and Crysede,"

> But canstow playen racket to and fro,
> Nettle in, dokke out; now this,
>   now that, Pandare?

showing that the racquet was in use at the day when this poem was written. But racquets were not suddenly brought into being. Early balls were hard — stuffed with wool or hair; it is much more likely to have been sheer physical necessity, rather than any exact knowledge of the principles of the lever, or of dynamics, which caused tennis devotees to devise a substitute for the bare palm. Players began by using gloves and then passed on to the art of stretching gut strings, similar to those which were used on their zebecs or violins, over the face of the glove. When in action, the hand would stretch these strings tightly, so as to form the racquet face. This is why the word *"racken,"* meaning to "stretch," is considered to be such a likely derivation. The handle was quickly added, possibly with some idea of extra leverage, and as gut strings were somewhat expensive, a light framework of wood came to be used, with parchment stretched tightly over the surface.

This use of these parchment battledores caused such a demand to arise for this commodity that, as might have been foreseen, the price went up by leaps and bounds. But the result to posterity was disastrous. It must be remembered in passing that tennis became so popular in France, especially in Paris, about the end of the 15th century and onwards, that it is on record that over 1,800 courts were to be found in the city of Paris — a number which must be received with some little caution.

Be this as it may, disaster came in that priceless manuscripts, whose owners did not recognize their true value, were sold for the purpose of making racquet heads. Historic records have it, in the

34

memoirs of M. Chatelain, that one of his friends, a man of letters, had played *La Longue Paûme* with a *battoir* (battledore) on which were legible some fragments of the lost decades of Livy; and that these fragments came from an apothecary who had obtained several volumes of the same author on vellum from certain religieuses, Nuns, probably, of Fontrevault who, in turn, had ignorantly sold them to a *battoir* maker.

Moncton, Pastimes in Times Past

With such an example before him, it was doubtless some forerunner of the " learn as you play " educators who developed the scheme of painting or impressing the letters of the alphabet on the wooden battledore " for children to learn their letters by." One lexicographer indeed calls the battledore a horn-book " because it has the same shape; it

Sketch showing both sides of a wooden battledore found in Wales

may be conjectured — perhaps reasonably — that as the use of letters increased, the battledore was reduced to a more portable size, covered with horn, and thenceforth called either the horn-book or battledore." So much for the wooden battledores, one of which is sketched on page 35. The paper battledore, illustrated on page 39, which was folded

3 Battledore and Shuttlecock.

From "Youthful Sports" edition of 1804, published by Darton and Harvey, London

to make two leaves and a flap, not only gave room for more lesson material but likewise, when made of stiff paper, was strong enough (according to Tuer), when so folded, to bat the shuttlecock (a cork stuck with feathers). It is difficult to believe that it served this purpose with anything like the success of its more sturdy namesake, but anyone who has observed the uses to which schoolboys can put their books when at play will readily understand the infinite possibilities of even a paper battledore. Another, and what seems to this writer, more logical reason for the name battledore, as applied to the folded paper or cardboard, is that, when unfolded for use as a lesson-book, it was the shape of the wooden battledore, or hornbook, minus the handle. In this connection, Mr. George Plimpton, in *The Hornbook and Its Use in America,* wrote as follows:

> Down through the centuries the hornbook gradually modified its form, finally losing its handle. With paper and print more available, cardboard A B C's took the place of the hornbook. The last illustration shown is that of a battledore book, which is obviously an outgrowth of the hornbook.

Battledores as lesson-books, then, represent the second stage in the development of children's books. As recorded in Tuer's *History of the Horn-book,* the inventor of the folding cardboard battledore was Benjamin

Collins and the date is fixed by his account books as 1746. He speaks of it as "my own invention" and the records show that between the years of 1770 and 1780 he sold more than a hundred thousand copies. The earliest battledores were covered with gilt-embossed Dutch paper. The inner, or lesson side, was generally varnished (an eighteenth-century method of coping with those still grubby little fingers). Later the colored Dutch paper was omitted as were also The Lord's Prayer and the Exorcism. Finally both sides were printed, and then the first series of readers was under way — for although all of them gave first place to the alphabet, the rest of the contents varied greatly both as to text and illustrations. Many printers issued battledores, most of the early specimens given titles such as *The Royal Battledore, The London New Battledore, The New Improved Battledore, The Good Child's Battledore, The Infant's Battledore,* and so on. Of these, Mr. Wilbur Macey Stone (the well-known collector), in a letter written but a few months before his death to acknowledge the receipt of some battledore reproductions with which

The ROYAL BATTLEDORE: Being the first Introductory Part of the Circle of the Sciences, &c. Publish'd by the KING's AUTHORITY. LONDON: Printed by J. Newbery, in St. Paul's Church-Yard, and B. Collins, in Sarum, Pr. 2d. Also the Royal Primer, or second Book for Children, Price 3d. bound, adorn'd with Cuts.

The Royal Battledore, printed by John Newbery,
on paper suggesting " flowery and gilt "

the author was then concerned, commented as follows:

What a very interesting thing to have reprinted some of the Battledores! And they are excellent facsimiles. Thank you *much* for the two you sent me.

I have quite a handful of the original issues

8 of the Alnwick: Davison issue
2 of the Penryn: Whitehorn issue
2 of the Nottingham: Wright issue
6 misc. issues
2 of Banbury: Rusher

all acquired 20 to 30 years ago at about a shilling each. My choicest one is an American issue, " The Uncle's Present," Phila: Jacob Johnson c — 1810, four leaves, all engraved, English street cries.

From the single, folded sheet of paper or cardboard of the early battledores — which had begun to decline in popularity and gave way altogether by the middle of the nineteenth century — it was but a step to the addition of an extra fold and thence to the extra leaves which but foreshadowed the spellers and real little lesson-books — but that is another story!

Six Centuries of the Horn-book
in Prose and Poetry

✣

Quan a chyld to scole xal set be,
  A bok hym is browt,
Naylyd on a brede of tre,
That men callyt an abece
  Pratylych i-wrout.

14th Century Ms. in the British Museum

Moth: Yes, yes; he teaches boys the hornbook.
  What is a, b, spelt backward with the horn on
  his head?
             Shakespeare, *Love's Labours Lost*

    Here
The letters may be read, through the horn,
That make the story perfect.

                 Ben Jonson, *Volpone*

Matters of Chiefe importance are in hast,
And for more speed dispatched by the horne,
Great light a Lanthorne, made of horne, doth cast,
Which with a candle in dark night is borne.
  When little children first are brought to schoole
A Horne-booke is a necessarie toole.

*Nicholas Breton, Cornucopiæ: Pasquil's Night
Cap, Or an Antidot for the Headache.* 1612

For a peny you may buy a dish of Coffee to quicken
your stomach and refresh your Spirits. For a peny
you may buy the hardest book in the world, and
which at some time or other hath posed the great-
est Clerks in the Land, viz. an Hornbook; the
making up of which Book imployeth above thirty
trades.

Henry Peacham, *The Worth of a Peny:*
or, A Caution to keep Money. 1664

And, having so the child's affection won,
(He saith) Sweet Lad, come, and thy Horn-booke
  con.
And so the A B C he first is taught;
From that to spelling, he is after brought;
And, being right instructed for to spell,
He learns his Sillables and Vowells well.
Then, with due teaching he doth well consider
By's Master's rule how he may put together.
The Horn-booke having at his fingers end,
Unto the Primer he doth next ascend.

      .   .   .

So, "from the Horne-booke" we must first incline
Before we can attain to things divine.
And, as the Bible is the well of preaching,
Even so the Horn-booke is the ground of teaching.

Hornbye's *Horn-Book.* 1622

    Thus much for artificial Babes; and now
To those who are in years but such, I bow
  My Pen to teach them what the Letters be,
And how they may improve their A, B, C.
Nor let my pretty Children them despise;
All needs must there begin, that would be wise

A silver horn-book said to have been owned by Queen Elizabeth

Nor let *them* fall under Discouragement,
Who at their Horn-book stick, and time hath spent
Upon that A, B, C, while others do
Into their Primer, or their Psalter go.
Some Boys with difficulty do begin,
Who in the end, the Bays, and Lawrel win.

> J. B. (John Bunyan) *A Book for Boys and Girls: or Country Rhimes for Children.* 1686

What other books there are in English of the kind above-mentioned[1] fit to engage the liking of children and tempt them to read, I do not know, but am apt to think, that children, being generally delivered over to the method of schools, where the fear of the rod is to inforce, and not any pleasure of the employment to invite them to learn, this sort of useful books, amongst the number of silly ones that are of all sorts, yet have had the fate to be neglected; and nothing that I know has been considered, of this kind, out of the ordinary road of the horn-book, primer, psalter, Testament and Bible.

> John Locke, *Thoughts on Education.* 1691

Hail ancient Book, most venerable Code,
Learning's first Cradle and its last Abode!
The Huge unnumbered Volumes which we see,
By lazy Plagiaries are stol'n from thee:
Yet future Times to thy sufficient Store
Shall ne'er presume to add one Letter more.

Thee will I sing in comely Wainscot bound,
And Golden Verge enclosing thee around;

[1] i.e. Aesop's *Fables* or *Reynard the Fox.*

44

The back of the "Queen Elizabeth" horn-book. The silver filigree is underlaid with red silk

The faithful Horn before, from Age to Age,
Preserving thy invaluable Page;

> Thomas Tickell, *Poem in Praise of the Horn-book.* 1728

Our parents yet exert a prudent care
To feed our minds with proper fare;
And wisely store the nursery by degrees
With wholesome learning, yet acquired with ease.
Neatly secured from being soil'd or torn,
Beneath a pane of thin translucent horn,
A book (to please us at a tender age
'Tis called a book, though but a single page)
Presents the prayer the Saviour deigned to teach,
Which children use, and parsons — when they
    preach.

> William Cowper, *Tirocinium, or a Review of Schools.* 1784

Inadventurous, unstirred by impulses of practical ambition. I was capable of sitting twenty years teaching infants the hornbook, turning silk dresses, and making children's frocks.

> Charlotte Brontë, *Vilette.* 1853

There were no children's books, properly so called, except the ballads, chap-books brought round by pedlars, often far from edifying, and the plunge from the horn-book into general literature was, to say the least of it, bracing.

> Charlotte M. Yonge, *Love and Life, an Old Story in Eighteenth Century Costume.* 1880

46

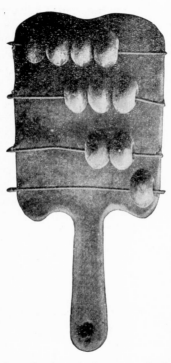

A horn-book with abacus on the back

From the earliest periods we find injunctions imposed upon the clergy that they should be careful to teach the people the Creed, the Lord's Prayer and the Ten Commandments in their own tongue . . . but in days when books were scarce, and when few could read, little could be done towards giving to the people at large this intelligent acquaintance with the Services except by oral instruction of the kind indicated. Yet the writing-rooms of the Monasteries did what they could towards multiplying books for the purpose; and some provision was made, even for the poorest, by means of hornbooks, on which the Lord's Prayer, the Creed and the Angelic Salutation were written. Whilst these hornbooks were thus provided for the poor, the Scriptorium of the Monastery also provided Prymers in English and Latin for those who could not afford the expensive luxury of a book. The Latin Prymers are well known under the name of " Books of Hours."

The Annotated Book of Common Prayer,
Edited by the Rev. Henry Blunt, D.D.
1893

Few people have ever seen a horn-book. The horn-book, which is not a book at all, but a little handled tablet of oak, on which is mounted a printed sheet containing the alphabet, short syllables, and the Lord's Prayer, faced with a thin pane of protective horn — hence its name — was used in days when books were scarce to teach little children the first rudiments of learning.

In olden times these tablets, some of which had the alphabet only, took the place of the spelling book, and were in use in every dame's school. Later on, when paper and print became cheapened, the horn-book was elbowed out of existence by the primer or spelling book.

If fortunate enough to unearth a horn-book, you may be glad to know that it is a thing of price and coveted by collectors.

From a publisher's announcement of Tuer's *History of the Horn-book* which appeared in *Horn-Book Jingles,* by Mrs. Arthur Gaskin. 1896

Little articles, like horn-books, rattles, mugs, intended for work-a-day human use, at first crude and simple in workmanship . . . are apt, as time goes by, to become more and more delicate and curious. As long, that is, as they are made by hand (so that a man can put his pleasure as well as his labour into them) and are not turned out by the thousand from a machine, which may have beauty and unfailing skill, but is sense-less. In any case, they remain lively little reminders of their own day and fashion and are well worth a close examination when found. . . .

Walter de la Mare in *Come Hither,* 1923

✠

Horn-book: The Horn-book was the Primer of our ancestors—their established means of learning the elements of English Literature. It consisted of a single leaf, containing on one side

the alphabet large and small — in black letters
or in Roman — and perhaps a small regiment
of monosyllables, and a copy of the Lord's Prayer;
and the leaf was usually set in a frame of wood
with a slice of diaphanous horn in front — hence
the name horn-book. Gradually there was a
handle to hold it by and this handle had usually
a hole for a string, whereby the apparatus was
slung to the girdle of the scholar. In a " View
of the Beau Monde" published 1731, a lady
is described as " dressed like a child, in a bodice-
coat, and leading strings, with a horn-book held
to her side."

Chambers, *The Book of Days*

Horn-book: A leaf of paper containing the alphabet (often with the addition of the ten digits,
some elements of spelling, and the Lord's Prayer)
protected by a thin plate of translucent horn,
and mounted on a tablet of wood with a pro-
jecting piece for a handle. A simpler and later
form of this, consisting of the tablet without the
horn covering, on a piece of stiff cardboard
varnished, was also called a Battledore.

Murray's *New English Dictionary*

The Horn-book in Title
and Mark

The earliest work in which the word "horn-book" appears to have been used as a title is *The Guls Horne-booke:* Imprinted at London by R.S. 1609. In this satire which takes the form of rules for conduct of the gallant, the prologue reads as follows: "A Horne-booke have I invented because I would have you well schooled, Powles is your Walke, but this is your Guid: if it lead you right thanke me; if astray, men will beare with your errors, because you are Guls. Fare-well. J.D.

The latest use of "horn-book," unless a still more recent one has escaped an eye somewhat on the watch for it, is to be found in the magazine *Antiques* where an illustration of a horn-book has been used with the departmental heading (set in old type) "The Hornbook for Collectors" followed, appropriately enough, by a subtitle, "The ABCs of Staffordshire." (*Antiques,* February, 1942)

Between this oldest and newest uses of the horn-book in titles are a number of others, a few of which are listed below.

POETASTER'S HORN-BOOK — in No. 93 of *The Connoisseur* (London, 1757) in which a proposed publication is described, concluding as follows: "The whole to be illustrated with examples from the modern poets. This elaborate work will be published about the middle of winter under the title of The Rhymer's Plaything, or Poetaster's Horn-Book; since there is nothing necessary to form such a poet except teaching him his letters."

THE BATTLE OF THE HORN-BOOKS — A political satire, published in Dublin in 1774, dealing with public persons of the period from which the following brief passage is quoted because of its connection with the mention on page 35 of the interchangeable use of battledore and hornbook. "A Lad of Blood might play at quoits, shuttlecock, or duck and drake, with his Hornbook, and it still continued bright and clean; whereas the book of a mean-spirited little fellow, tho' kept with the nicest care, had always a soiled look, and the letters were hardly distinguishable."

DEATH AND DOCTOR HORNBOOK — Burns's poem, "Ye ken Jock Hornbook i the Cha-chan . . ."

A HORN-BOOK FOR A PRINCE, *or the A B C of Politics* (in verse). London, 1811.

THE PARSON'S HORN-BOOK — anonymous theological and political satire, published in 1831.

THE HORN-BOOK OF STORMS — Henry Piddington's guide to the track of storms in the Southern Indian Ocean and Arabian Sea. Plates of horn were etched so as to indicate storm circles; when laid over any part of the charts in the book they define the storm circles within a given area. The plates were enclosed in a pocket in the back of the book. Calcutta, 1847.

HORNBOOK JINGLES — a hand-lettered book of rhymes about horn-books and children, illustrated by the author, Mrs. Arthur Gaskin. London, 1896.

Reproduction of the rose, thistle and acorn design stamped on a leather horn-book

THE HORNBOOK SERIES—A Handbook of American Constitutional Law, by Henry Campbell Black. 1897.

GINN AND COMPANY—*The Athenæum Press.* One of America's finest publishers of textbooks uses the horn-book as its trademark. As may be seen in the reproduction, a hand holds the horn-book, surrounded by leaves of the oak and laurel "representing strength, reliability, and honor, always inseparable from any worthy activity in the cause of education."

THE HORN BOOK MAGAZINE—Founded in 1924 as a part of the work for The Bookshop for Boys and Girls, The Women's Educational and Industrial Union. Published currently as a bimonthly under the ægis of its original editor, Bertha E. Mahony, by the Horn Book, Inc., Boston, Massachusetts.

Sources

BOOKS

Blunt, The Rev. Henry [Editor]. *The Annotated Book of Common Prayer, Being an Historical Ritual and Theological Commentary on the Devotional System of the Church of England.* New York: E. P. Dutton & Co., 1893.

Carter, Thomas Francis. *The Invention of Printing in China and Its Spread Westward.* New York: Columbia University Press, 1925.

Chambers, Robert [Editor]. *The Book of Days.* London: Chambers, 1863. [Philadelphia: J. B. Lippincott Co.]

Earle, Alice Morse. *Child Life in Colonial Days.* New York: The Macmillan Co., 1899.

Field, Mrs. E. M. *The Child and His Book.* London: Wells, Garner, Darton Co., 1891.

Garnett, Richard, and Gosse, Edmund. *English Literature, An Illustrated Record.* New York: The Macmillan Co., 1905.

Gaskin, Mrs. Arthur. *Hornbook Jingles.* London: The Leadenhall Press, 1896.

Gress, Edmund G. *The American Handbook of Printing.* New York: Oswald Publishing Co., 1907.

McMurtrie, Douglas C. *The Book.* New York: Covici, Friede, 1937.

Moncton, O. Paul. *Pastimes in Times Past.* London: The West Strand Publishing Co., Ltd., 1913. [Philadelphia: J. B. Lippincott Co.]

Perry, The Rev. William Stevens. *History of the American Episcopal Church 1587–1883.* Boston: James R. Osgood & Co., 1885.

Plimpton, George A. *The Hornbook and Its Use in America.* [Booklet, reprinted from an address before the American Antiquarian Society.] Boston: Ginn and Co., 1916.

Quennell, Marjorie and C. H. B. *The History of Everyday Things in England.* London: B. T. Batsford, Ltd., 1937.

Stone, Wilbur Macey. *Four Centuries of Children's Books.* [Booklet printed for the first display of these books from the Collection of Wilbur Macey Stone.] Boston: The Public Library of the City of Boston, 1928.

Tapley, Harriet Silvester. *Salem Imprints, 1768–1825.* Salem, Massachusetts: The Essex Institute, 1927.

Tuer, Andrew W. *History of the Horn-book.* London: The Leadenhall Press, 1897. [New York: Charles Scribner's Sons.]

Wroth, Lawrence C. *The Colonial Printer.* Portland, Maine: The Southworth-Anthoensen Press, 1938.

PERIODICALS

Bibliographic: Papers on Books, Their History and Art. Volume III, 1896 [London].

Independent, The, August 1, 1912.

Mentor, April 1928.

Nation, The, August 13, 1896.

Walford's Antiquarian Magazine, October 1882.
[London.]

ILLUSTRATIONS

For permission to reproduce on many pages of this
book illustrations from other publications, the author acknowledges her indebtedness to Charles
Scribner's Sons for those used on the endleaves and
title page, and on pages 3, 7, 9, 17, 21, 28, 30, 31,
32, 35, 39, 43, 45, 53, 57 [all of these are from
Tuer's *History of the Horn-book,* long since out of
print]; to The Ronald Press Company for the Map
which follows page 18; to the Loring Collection,
Department of Graphic Arts, Harvard College
Library, for the design of the eighteenth century
Dutch paper used on the cover and on the battledore on page 39; to Ginn and Company for the
illustrations on pages 25, 47, 54 [taken from *Marks
of Merit, Together With An Article on Hornbooks
and Their Use in America,* by George A. Plimpton].

*Decoration, about quarter size,
printed on the back of the horn-
book shown on page 17*